THE YOUNG ASTRONOMER

Sheila Snowden

Edited by Lynn Myring

Designed by Roger Priddy

Illustrated by Martin Newton,
Rob McCaig, Rex Archer, Kuo Kang Chen

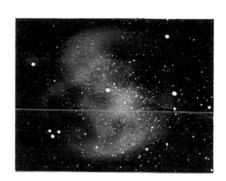

Contents

2 Starting astronomy
4 Choosing equipment
6 Constellations
8 The whirling sky
10 Stars in space
12 Types of stars
14 Galaxies, star clusters and nebulae
16 Life story of the stars
17 The planets
21 The Moon
24 The Sun
26 Eclipses
28 Comets and meteors
30 Going further
32 Index

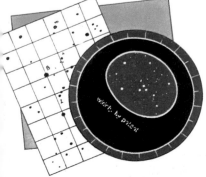

Starting astronomy

You do not need to have any special equipment at all to begin astronomy, although binoculars are very useful. What you really need is the patience to study the sky regularly and to note what you see and then find out more about it. It is a good idea to join a local astronomical society as they organize observational outings and the members will be able to give you lots of help. It is not worth buying a telescope until you have learned your way around the sky. They are very expensive and more difficult to use and carry about than binoculars.

These two pages explain how to go about observing the night sky, with tips on getting comfortable and making notes. The rest of the book explains many of the things that you are likely to see.

A big problem for all astronomers is unwanted light from street lamps, cars and houses. It makes the sky very bright, blotting out lots of stars, but you will still be able to observe the Moon, the main constellations and the four brightest planets.

It takes about half an hour for your eyes to adapt to the dark. Once they are night-adapted you will be able to see more stars. Red light does not interfere too much with night-adapted sight, so use a torch covered in red cellophane if you want to look at a star map or make notes while observing.

Star maps

Before you go out observing, look at a star map to see which stars are visible and where in the sky you can find them.

A simple star map that shows the main stars and the brightest constellations is the best choice if you are a beginner. Complicated maps can be confusing as some of the stars on them can only be seen with a telescope. The most useful kind of star map is

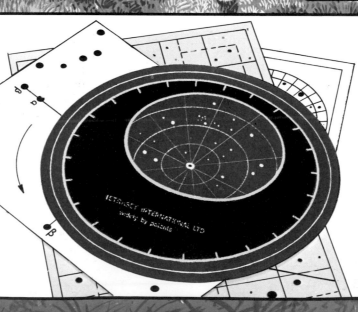

called a planisphere. It is a circular map of the stars, with the 12 months of the year printed round the edge. A moveable overlay with the 24 hours of the day printed on it goes on top of the map. You line up the time of your observation with the date, and a window in the overlay reveals the stars visible at that time and on that day.

Choosing an observing site

If you live in a town, you will be astonished by the blackness of the sky and the brilliance of the stars in the countryside. A hill makes a good observation site as you get a clearer view of the sky from higher up. Choose and visit your site in daylight and work out where north, south, east and west are. Use land marks such as trees or houses to help you remember which way is which when you return in the dark.

Seeing conditions

The weather and air conditions will affect how much you can see. Clouds, haze, dust in the air and mist will all make it difficult to observe very much. Another problem is turbulence – the movement of currents of air in the atmosphere. This makes the stars look as if they

Path of light from a star travels straight in space but seems to wobble through the air.

are twinkling and if it is very bad it can make them almost dance about. When conditions are poor it is better to use binoculars, or even the naked eye, as high magnification will make observations worse. Astronomers call these conditions "seeing" and rate it on a scale of 1 (very good) to 5 (very bad).

Astronomy in comfort

Nights can be very chilly, even in summer and you will not enjoy astronomy much if you are cold and uncomfortable. Always wear more clothes than you think you need – a hat and gloves with the finger tips cut off are often necessary, and a blanket or sleeping bag will keep your legs warm. If you are using binoculars a deckchair makes a comfortable seat and a small stool is useful with a telescope.

Making notes

By making notes of your observations you will soon build up a record of astronomical objects and events. Write down the weather and seeing conditions and make a note of the Moon and other light. Also note the place, date and time of your observation. Astronomers use a special time system called Universal Time (UT) so that observation from all over the world can be compared. Universal Time is the same as Greenwich Mean Time (GMT).

Record anything you can see, noting details such as size, colour, brilliance, position in relation to other stars and movement, if any. When observing constellations, count the number of stars.

This picture shows some of the things that it is worth remembering to take out when you are observing. A note book and pencil to record observations, and a camera if you want to take photographs. A compass so that you know which direction you are looking in. A watch so you can note the time. A red light torch for reading star maps and a hot drink to keep you going.

Choosing equipment

With good binoculars you can see about ten times more stars than are visible to the naked eye, many details of the Moon's surface and even the planet Jupiter and some of its moons. Of course, a telescope will show you more, but this is not really an advantage if you are a beginner. It is confusing to see too many stars while you are still learning to recognize the main constellations. Astronomical telescopes are also very expensive and as they give an upside-down image, they are not much good for anything other than astronomy. Ordinary, terrestrial telescopes are not worth buying especially for astronomy – binoculars would be better.

Binoculars

Binoculars are sold in many sizes and powers, which are indicated by a pair of numbers, such as 8×30, 10×50 or 20×80. The first number tells you by how many times the binoculars will magnify an object. The second number is the measurement in millimetres across the front (or objective) lenses of the binoculars.

Big powerful binoculars are heavy and very difficult to hold still when you are observing. Try out some 8×40s, 7×50s and 10×50s to see which are the most comfortable for you. 10×50 is about the largest size you can use without having to mount your binoculars on a tripod. A camera tripod is good for this and will help you to observe even if using smaller binoculars, as it keeps them very still.

Focusing controls

Eye piece lenses

These are the front or objective lenses. Big lenses gather more light, making the image clear and bright, but they are heavy.

Even if you are going to buy a telescope later on, you will still need binoculars as they are better for some kinds of observations. Binoculars are good for sweeping the sky to look for comets or novae (exploding stars) and also for seeing faint, fuzzy objects such as nebulae (gas clouds) and galaxies.

Field of view

Another advantage of binoculars is that they have a wider field of view than a telescope. This means that you can see more of the sky through them, which is useful while you are learning the stars. A telescope will show you only part of a constellation, probably only one or two stars. These pictures show the constellation Orion as it is seen by the naked eye, then by binoculars and lastly through a small telescope.

Naked eye view

Binocular view

Telescope view

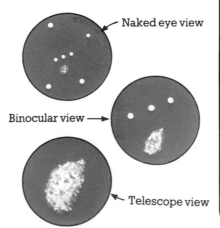

Terrestrial telescopes

If you have an ordinary (terrestrial) telescope it is worth trying it out for astronomy. You will need to mount it on a tripod. It will give a higher magnification than binoculars, but the image may be less clear as they are not specially made for use at night.

Astronomical telescopes

This is a small telescope called a spotting-scope or finder-scope. It has a wide field of view to help you line up the main telescope with what you want to observe.

This picture shows a typical newtonian reflecting telescope.

There is no lens at this end of a reflector as it has a mirror at the bottom of the tube.

Reflectors and refractors

There are two main kinds of astronomical telescope to choose between: refractors which gather light through lenses, like binoculars, and reflectors which use a mirror to collect the light. Both kinds have changeable eye pieces that use lenses to give different magnifications. The diagrams on the left show how light passes through both kinds of telescope. The main picture shows a reflector.

Refractors are much more expensive than reflectors, so most amateur astronomers use reflectors. Many build their own as this is the cheapest way of getting a big telescope. There are several designs of reflecting telescope, and one of the most common is called a newtonian.

Objective lens   Eye piece

Mirror

Eye piece

Mirror

The magnification eye pieces fit on here.

Mirror is in here.

This telescope is standing on an equatorial mounting.

Mountings

All telescopes are too heavy and big to be held by hand. They have to be mounted on a stand and many are sold complete with one. There are two kinds of stand – altazimuth mounts and equatorial mounts.

An altazimuth mount is the simpler kind. It allows you to move the telescope up and down (altitude) and from side to side (azimuth). Camera tripods have altazimuth mounts.

Equatorial mounts are more sophisticated, and more difficult to set up, as they have to be aligned with the Earth's polar axis. They allow you to follow the curved path of a star across the sky with just one movement.

Telescope accessories

Barlow Lens

Star diagonal

You can buy different eye pieces which give various powers of magnification. Most telescopes are supplied with two or three. A device called a Barlow Lens will increase by two or three times the magnification power of any eye piece. A star diagonal is a right-angle shaped eye piece which lets you look at stars high in the sky without having to bend down very low.

Telescope sizes

A telescope's power is not measured by its magnification, but by the size of the mirror (in a reflector) or lens (in a refractor) which is used. The larger the mirror or lens, the more light the telescope can collect. It is the amount of light which makes the image bright and clear. You will get a larger image with a big telescope and also be able to use higher magnification and see more details. It is not really worth buying a reflector smaller than 100mm (4in) or a refractor smaller than 75mm (3in).

Choosing a telescope

Choosing a telescope can be very difficult. Look at advertisements in astronomy magazines and send away for catalogues. Try out other people's telescopes and ask their advice. You may be able to get one second-hand from an astronomer who is getting a larger telescope. Refractors are slightly easier to look after than reflectors which need to have their mirrors re-aligned and recoated with reflecting aluminium occasionally. Telescopes are delicate instruments and need to be handled with care, always following the maker's instructions.

There is a new kind of telescope, called a catadioptric, which uses a combination of mirrors and lenses. These are more compact than a refractor or reflector of the same size, but they are also more expensive.

Constellations

In ancient times astronomers grouped bright stars together into patterns called constellations, which they named after people, gods and animals. We still use these constellations today along with a few new ones, such as Telescopium the Telescope. Each constellation has a Latin name but many are better known by an English equivalent. Some have nicknames too, such as the northern constellation Ursa Major which is known as the Plough or Big Dipper although its proper name in English is the Great Bear.

The maps on these two pages show the constellations you will be able to see during the course of a year. There is one map for the northern hemisphere and one for the southern hemisphere. You will not be able to see all of the stars on your map at any one time.

Northern hemisphere

The names of constellations are shown in light type, with the names of the brighter stars in heavier type. Some of these stars are mentioned later in this book.

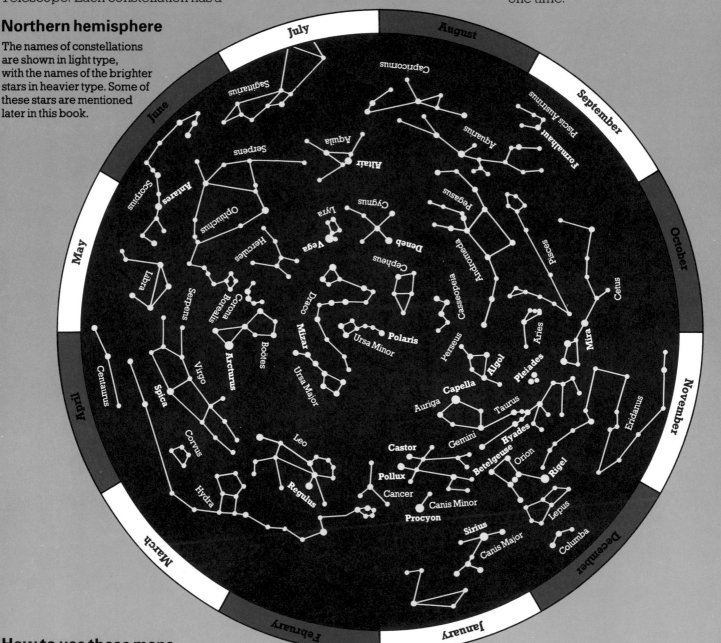

How to use these maps

Choose the map appropriate for the hemisphere that you are in. Turn it so that the current month is at the bottom. The lower half and middle of the map then shows the stars you will see if you look south in the northern hemisphere and north in the southern hemisphere at midnight.

Naming stars

Most stars are known by the name of the constellation that they are in and a Greek letter. The brightest star in a constellation is given the first letter of the alphabet, alpha, the next brightest the second letter, beta, and so on. The brightest star of the constellation Canis Major is called Alpha Canis Major, or α C. Maj. for short. There are only 24 letters in the Greek alphabet, so if a constellation has more than 24 stars those fainter than omega are numbered.

Most of the very brilliant stars also hav

Spotting the constellations

When you first go outside to look for a constellation, it may seem impossible to pick out their patterns from the mass of stars in the sky. They look much more spread out and less obvious in the sky than on a map. Once you have spotted a constellation, however, you will probably be able to find it again quite easily. It is important to learn to recognize the shapes of the constellations as they change their positions in the sky during the night. Also some are visible all year while others are seasonal and can be seen for only a few months. You can find out more about star movements on pages 8 and 9. Use the constellations that you know to help you find others nearby in the sky. Some good ones to begin with are Ursa Major, Cygnus and Cassiopeia in the northern hemisphere, Crux in the southern and Orion, Pegasus, Virgo, Canis Major, Gemini and Aquila from both.

Southern hemisphere

The names of constellations are shown in light type, with the names of the brighter stars in heavier type. Some of these stars are mentioned later in this book.

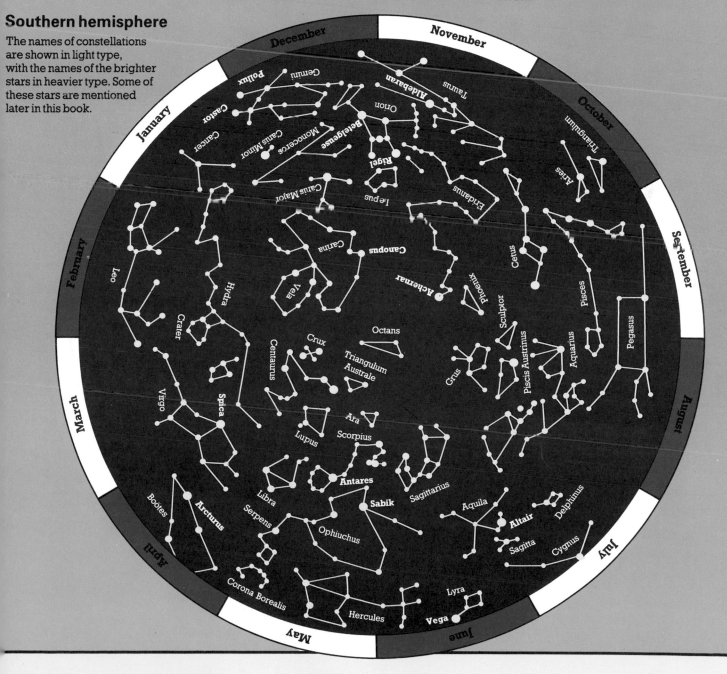

their own names, quite apart from their constellation names. α C. Maj. is also known as Sirius, a name of Greek origin. Many have English nicknames too – Sirius is called the Dog Star.

Here are the Greek letters and names.

α	Alpha	η	Eta	ν	Nu	τ	Tau
β	Beta	θ	Theta	ξ	Xi	υ	Upsilon
γ	Gamma	ι	Iota	ο	Omicron	φ	Phi
δ	Delta	κ	Kappa	π	Pi	χ	Chi
ε	Epsilon	λ	Lambda	ρ	Rho	ψ	Psi
ζ	Zeta	μ	Mu	σ	Sigma	ω	Omega

The whirling sky

One of the things which makes star spotting seem difficult at first is the fact that the stars appear to be moving all the time. They keep their positions in relation to each other but appear in a slightly different place each evening and drift across the sky during the night. Some stars stay in the sky all night while others set after a few hours and new ones rise to take their places.

This drift is very slow and is not obvious if you are just standing looking at the stars. However, a telescope magnifies star drift, so that a star moves out of sight within a few moments and you will have to track it across the sky.

These pages show how and why stars seem to move in this way.

Star drift

Here is an experiment which will show you a star's nightly drift across the sky. Pick out a bright star or constellation and stand somewhere so that it lines up with an immobile landmark, such as a tree. Note the time and return to the same spot an hour later.

You will find that the stars have moved to the west of the landmark but without changing their positions in relation to each other. If you look out for the same stars over the next few days, you will find that they line up with your landmark four minutes earlier each night.

Photographing the stars

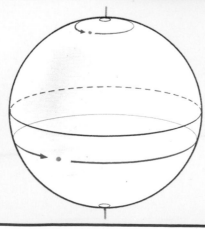

You can also show the movement of the stars by taking a photograph. You need a camera which allows you to keep the shutter open for as long as your finger is on the button, as you have to make a long exposure. Use a cable release if you have one. You also need to keep the camera very steady by mounting it on a tripod or by propping it up on a firm surface with some books.

Point the camera at some bright stars and leave the shutter open for about a minute or more according to your film speed. When you send the film to be developed, tell the processors that you have taken star pictures otherwise they may think that the frame is blank. The resulting photographs should show the stars as small curved trails in the sky. If you have used colour film you should be able to see the colours of the stars more clearly than you can with the naked eye.

Why stars drift

The apparent rotation of the celestial sphere makes the stars look as if they are spinning in circles around the celestial poles. The stars close to the poles move in small circles while those near the celestial equator move in large ones. Your view of the stars depends upon where you are on the Earth.

Skies from Earth's polar regions

From the north and south poles all the stars that you can see would wheel round in complete circles. None would rise and set. They would all be visible all of the night. The stars would circle round a central point directly overhead.

Mapping the sky

The movement of the stars across the sky makes them look as if they are fixed to the inside of a huge sphere which rotates around the Earth once a day. It was once thought that this actually happened, but even though we now know it doesn't, the idea of an imaginary sphere – called the celestial sphere – is still very useful. It shows what seems to be happening to the stars and helps astronomers make maps of the sky.

In order to pinpoint a place on Earth, geographers give it two co-ordinates in degrees of latitude and longitude. Astronomers do the same thing for stars by plotting lines of latitude and longitude on the celestial sphere. Celestial latitude is called "Declination" (or Dec. for short). Celestial longitude is called "Right Ascension" (or R.A. for short). Most star maps have lines of Dec. and R.A. marked on them.

Declination

Lines of Declination run around the celestial sphere parallel with the equator. A star's Declination is measured as an angle in degrees (°) and minutes ('). It tells you where a star is between the equator and the pole. A star north of the equator is given a positive angle of Declination, such as +45°6'. Stars south of the equator have negative angles.

The north and south poles and equator of the celestial sphere are directly above those of Earth.

Don't worry if you find the principles of Declination and Right Ascension difficult to follow. You do not have to understand them in order to find your way around the sky. You can probably find most stars just with a good star map.

Right Ascension

Lines of Right Ascension run round the celestial sphere from north to south passing through the poles. Right Ascension is marked in hours and minutes of time as it is related to the apparent rotation of the celestial sphere around the Earth. Lines of Right Ascension begin from a place called "the first point of Aries". This marks the Sun's apparent position on the sphere on 21 March each year.

Declination and Right Ascension are most useful if you have a telescope that is fitted with setting circles. These point the telescope to the correct place in the sky when set with a star's Declination and Right Ascension.

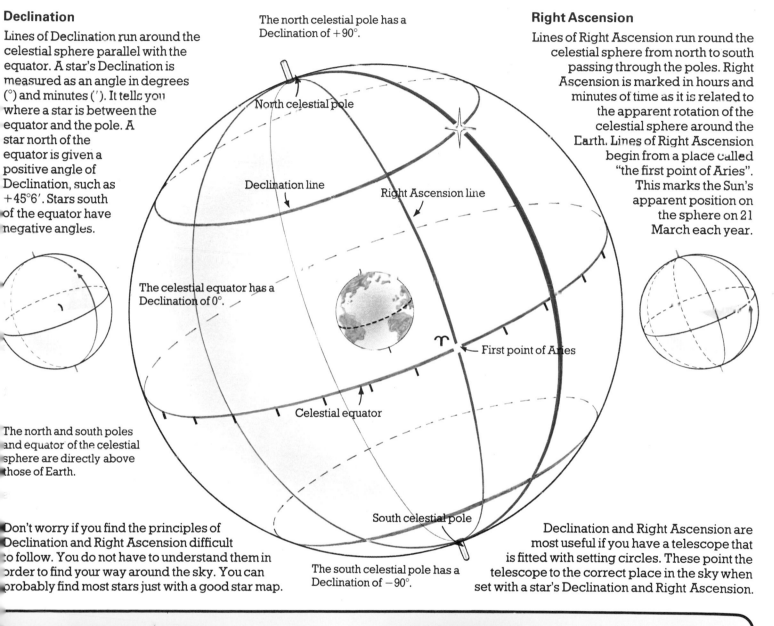

The north celestial pole has a Declination of +90°.

North celestial pole

Declination line

Right Ascension line

The celestial equator has a Declination of 0°.

First point of Aries

Celestial equator

South celestial pole

The south celestial pole has a Declination of −90°.

Skies from Earth's equatorial regions

Things are quite different from the equator. All of the stars would rise and set, moving in semi-circles round points north and south on the horizon. None would wheel round in complete circles or be visible for the whole night.

Skies from other places

From places on earth between the poles and the equator some stars rise and set and some circle the sky all night. The stars which circle the celestial poles and are visible all the time are called "circumpolar" stars.

Stars in space

The celestial sphere is a good way of showing how the stars seem to move, but it is not a true picture of what is happening. Really it is the Earth which is moving in space not the sky moving round Earth.

The stars seem to drift across the sky at night because the Earth is turning on its axis. This rotation turns the part of Earth you are on to face different parts of space over 24 hours. During the day you face the Sun and the Earth's rotation makes it seem to rise, cross the sky and then set. At night you face dark outer space and see the stars instead.

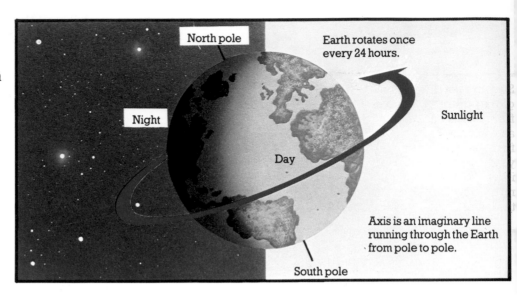

North pole

Earth rotates once every 24 hours.

Night

Sunlight

Day

Axis is an imaginary line running through the Earth from pole to pole.

South pole

The seasonal stars

As well as appearing to move across the sky during the night, the stars also change so that you see some different ones each month. Not all stars are seasonal in this way. The circumpolar stars, which do not rise and set during the night, are visible all year. It is the stars which do rise and set that change.

This happens because Earth orbits the Sun, taking a year to make its long journey through space. During its orbit, the dark night side of Earth faces out towards different parts of space,

as shown in the picture below. So we get a changing view of different stars over the months.

The stars that can be seen in June are on the same side of the sky as the Sun six months later in December. They are invisible then as they are in the daytime sky and the brilliant light of the Sun blots out their faint light. The stars "above" and "below" the Earth are the circumpolar stars which can be seen all year, but only from one hemisphere.

December stars

June stars

Distances in space

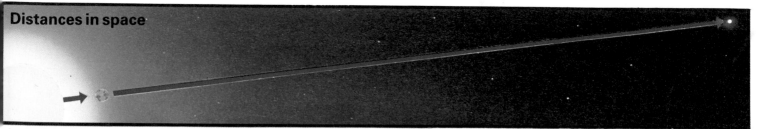

Stars are not stuck on the inside of a huge globe but are all different distances away from us. Distances in space are so vast that astronomers have had to invent a new unit for measuring them. It is called the light year. This is the distance that light travels in one year, which is about 10 million million km (6 million million mi). Light is the fastest thing in the Universe, travelling at 299,791 km (186, 238 mi) per second.

The closest star to our solar system is Proxima Centauri which is 4.2 light years away. Most stars are much more distant – there are only about 11 stars within 10 light years of us. Many are hundreds of light years away from us. Deneb, the brightest star of the constellation Cygnus, is probably more than 1,500 light years away (1,500 × 10 million million km).

As starlight takes time to reach us we are not really seeing a star as it is now, but as it was when the light first set out on its long journey across space. We see Proxima Centauri as it was 4.2 years ago and Deneb as it was 1,500 years ago. Looking at the stars is like looking back through time.

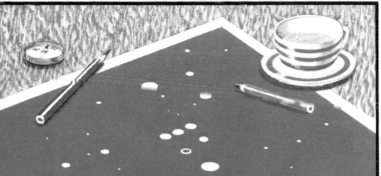

Star brilliance

◀ Stars are not all of the same brightness. Their brilliance is measured on a scale known as magnitude or Mag. for short. Bright stars are Mag. 1 or 2 and the very brightest have negative numbers. Sirius the most brilliant star in our sky is Mag. −1.4. The faintest stars visible to the naked eye are of Mag. 6. With binoculars you can see stars down to about Mag. 8 and a telescope will reveal stars of Mag. 12 or so.

Each step of magnitude indicates an increase in brightness of two and a half times. So a Mag. 1 star is two and a half times brighter than a Mag. 2 star, which in turn is two and a half times brighter than a Mag. 3 star and so on.

Stars actually have two different magnitudes. The first is their magnitude as they appear to us in the sky. This is called apparent magnitude and is what is shown on the maps. However, stars are not all the same distance away from Earth and those which are near appear brighter than those which are further away.

The second type of magnitude is a measure of a star's true brilliance and is called absolute magnitude. This compares stars with each other. Astronomers calculate a star's absolute magnitude by working out how bright it would appear in our sky if it were 32.6 light years away.

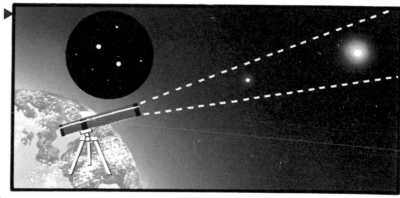

Constellations

The constellations are not real groupings of stars in space at all. The stars which we see as the constellation Orion, for example, vary between less than 500 light years and over 2,000 light years away from us. They just look like a connected group from Earth because the stars lie in the same direction and are close in apparent magnitude. A few stars may be genuinely close though. This diagram shows the constellation Orion as it looks in the sky and how the stars are really positioned in space.

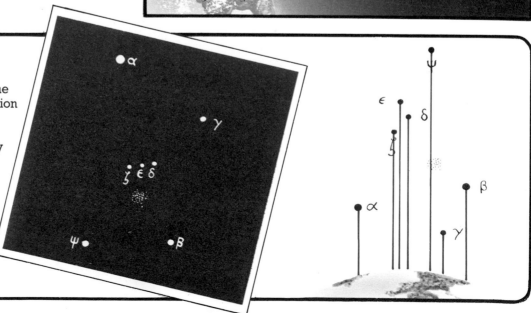

Types of stars

At first glance all stars look very much alike but with binoculars or a telescope you will see that they are different colours. You may even find that what looks like a single star to the naked eye, turns out to be two stars. These pages show some of the different kinds of stars astronomers have discovered.

Apart from the Sun, the stars are too distant to be studied in close up with the largest telescopes or even to be explored by spacecraft. However, astronomers can calculate a star's temperature, size, brilliance, chemical composition, distance from Earth and how it is moving in space, by analyzing starlight.

Star colours

Astronomers have found that most stars fall into a few main groups and they classify them by colour. Each class is called a spectral type and is identified by a letter. The main spectral types are shown in this chart.

A star's colour reflects its temperature, and both depend on the chemicals it is made from. The hottest stars are blue or white, the coolest red, with yellow and orange in between. Temperature is related to a star's absolute magnitude, or true brilliance, as the hotter the star the brighter it shines.

Type	O	B	A	F	G	K	M
Colour	Blue	Bluish White	White	Yellowish White	Yellow	Orange	Red
Temp °C	35,000	21,000	10,000	7,500	6,000	4,700	3,300
Main Chemicals	Helium	Helium	Hydrogen	Calcium	Metals	Hydro-carbons	Complex mix
Examples to spot	Zeta Orionis	Spica Achernar	Altair Sirius	Canopus Procyon	Sun Capella	Aldebaran Pollux	Arcturus Antares

Star sizes

This diagram compares the size of some bright stars which are shown on the star maps on pages 6 and 7 together with the Sun and Earth.

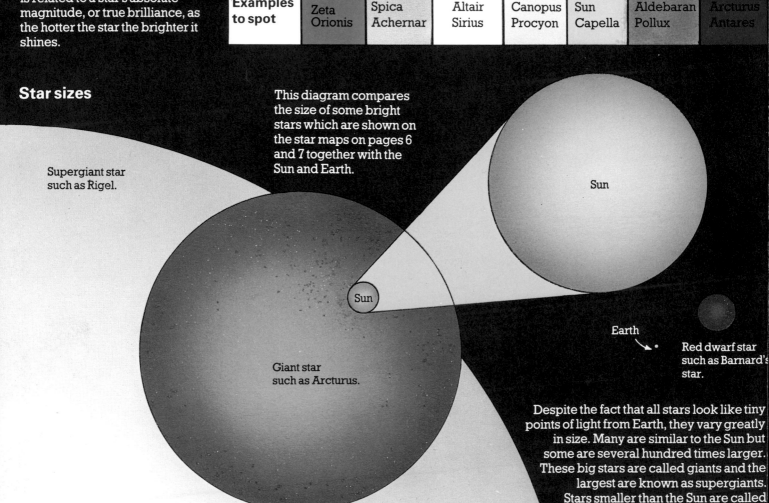

Supergiant star such as Rigel.

Sun

Sun

Giant star such as Arcturus.

Earth

Red dwarf star such as Barnard's star.

Despite the fact that all stars look like tiny points of light from Earth, they vary greatly in size. Many are similar to the Sun but some are several hundred times larger. These big stars are called giants and the largest are known as supergiants. Stars smaller than the Sun are called dwarf stars. Size also affects a star's absolute magnitude as large stars are brighter than smaller ones of the same colour and temperature

Double stars

The Sun is a single star but about half of the stars we can see from Earth are not lone stars at all. They are systems of two or more stars which orbit around each other, relatively close in space.

A pair of stars is known as a binary system. It often consists of two stars of different spectral types and sizes. If one is brighter it is called the primary and the fainter star is called the secondary. Some binary star systems can even be seen by the naked eye. One of these is the binary made up of the stars Mizar and Alcor, in the constellation of the Plough.

Star systems with more than two stars are called multiple systems. Some stars which appear to be binaries when seen through binoculars turn out to be multiple systems with a telescope. In the constellation Orion, the star Theta Orionis can be seen through a small telescope as four distinct stars, known as the Trapezium.

Most star maps indicate the stars which are binary or multiple systems so you can look up examples to search for and you will find a list of binary stars on page 30 of this book. There are also a few stars which seem to be binaries but which are not really. These are called optical doubles and occur because the stars lie along the same line of sight, in much the same way as constellations look as if they are groups of related stars.

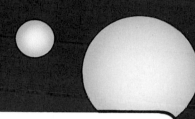

Variable stars

As you study the sky over a few weeks, you may be surprised to see that a few stars appear to change gradually in brilliance. This is because they are variable stars. A good star map will indicate stars which vary in magnitude.

You need to watch a variable star over a period of a few weeks or even months to see it go through a cycle of changes. It is also necessary to compare it with a nearby star which is not variable, so that you can tell whether it is getting fainter or brighter. There are several types of variable star and some have very regular and predictable cycles while others are erratic. This is because stars change in brightness for different reasons.

Pulsating variables

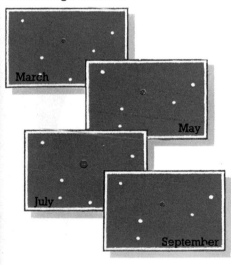

Many stars change in magnitude because they are changing physically in size and temperature. This usually happens to red giant stars which are at the end of their lives and have become unstable. They shrink and swell, giving off more light when large and less when small. These pulsating variables have long periods, taking between 100 to 400 days to go through a cycle. A good example is the red giant star Mira in the constellation Cetus. It changes over about 11 months from a bright Mag. 2 right down to Mag. 11 – too faint even to be seen with binoculars.

Eclipsing binaries

Some variable stars are not single stars at all but a binary system of two stars which appear to pass in front of each other as seen from Earth. As one star eclipses the other, it reduces the amount of light you can see. If the two stars are unequal in brilliance there will be two dips in magnitude. One when the bright primary eclipses the fainter secondary, and a bigger dip when the secondary eclipses the primary. This sort of variable star has a very regular cycle, usually of a few days or weeks. An example is Algol, in the constellation Perseus, which drops from Mag. 3.5 to 2.2 over a period of 50 hours.

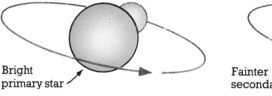
Bright primary star

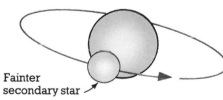
Fainter secondary star

Novae

The most exciting kind of variable star that you can hope to see is a nova. This is the extreme and unexpected brightening of a star and may look like the sudden appearance of a new star. Novae are uncommon – only about 25 have been seen this century, usually discovered by keen amateur astronomers.

A nova flares very suddenly, changing in apparent magnitude by between five and fifteen times – an increase of true brilliance of up to 100,000 times. The star then fades back to its original magnitude over several months, or even years if it became really bright. It is thought that novae are binary systems where gas from one star is dragged off by the other, (usually a white dwarf) causing violent nuclear reactions.

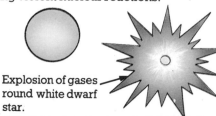
Explosion of gases round white dwarf star.

Galaxies, star clusters and nebulae

When searching the night sky, you will come across a few faint, fuzzy patches of hazy light. These are either nebulae, star clusters, the Milky Way or galaxies outside our own. The bright ones are usually marked on star maps and some are shown here.

Observing fuzzy objects

Wait for dark, moonless skies and good seeing conditions as these faint, hazy objects are easily blotted out by other lights. Binoculars or a small telescope are the best things to use for making observations as high magnification will not reveal very much detail anyway.

The best views are obtained by professional astronomers taking long exposure photographs using giant telescopes. These allow enough time for a good image to build up. You may find your own observations rather disappointing after looking at photographs and the pictures here. The images you observe will look small and vague.

The Milky Way

The largest and most obvious area of hazy diffuse light in the night sky is the **Milky Way**. It runs in a band across the sky passing through several constellations and can be seen from both hemispheres. Binoculars or a telescope will show you that it is made up of millions of stars, which look very crowded together. The Milky Way is a view along the plane of our Galaxy, in the directions of the red arrows on the pictures below. The Galaxy is a collection of about a hundred thousand million stars and is shaped rather like a catherine wheel firework. The Sun is positioned in one of the spiral arms about two thirds of the way out from the centre, shown by the red dots on the pictures. All the stars we can see are part of the Galaxy.

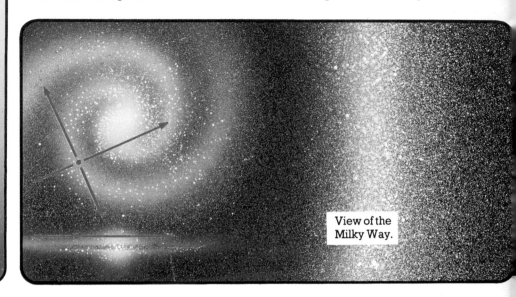

View of the Milky Way.

Galaxies

Our Galaxy is just one of the countless number which make up the Universe. Many other galaxies can be seen from Earth, a few with the naked eye. They just look like smudges of light, even with a telescope, as you are seeing the combined light of millions of stars. Their shapes are only clearly seen on long exposure photographs. Galaxies are not just scattered about the Universe, but grouped together in clusters. Our cluster, often called the Local Group, is quite small, containing about 20 galaxies in a radius of 2.5 million light years. Not all galaxies are spiral shaped, some are irregular, circular or elliptical.

The closest galaxies to us are two irregularly shaped mini-galaxies known as the Large and Small Magellanic Clouds. they are companions to our own Galaxy and can be seen only from the southern hemisphere.

This is the Andromeda Galaxy which is the most distant object visible to the naked eye. It is 2.2 million light years away and can be seen in the constellation Andromeda. It is a large spiral shaped galaxy, similar to our own.

A large cluster of several thousands of galaxies has been photographed in the constellation Virgo. It contains galaxies of all shapes and sizes and some of them can be seen with a small telescope although about 40 million lights years away.

Star clusters

There are two quite different types of star cluster. Open clusters are made up of bright young stars which have just formed from a nebula and are still relatively close together in space.

The Pleiades, pictured above, are an open cluster of bright young stars that can be seen in the constellation Taurus. With the naked eye you can see six or seven stars, many more with binoculars and, through a telescope it is difficult to count them. Although the stars look close together they are spread over a distance of about 15 light years.

The other type of star cluster is the globular cluster. These are much larger and further away from us than open clusters. In fact, globular clusters are not in the main part of the Galaxy at all, but scattered around its outer edges.

There are about a hundred known globular clusters, each containing up to a million stars. A few look like weak, faint stars to the naked eye and more are visible with binoculars. A telescope will show them as fuzzy patches and if large enough may even resolve some of the individual stars around the edges.

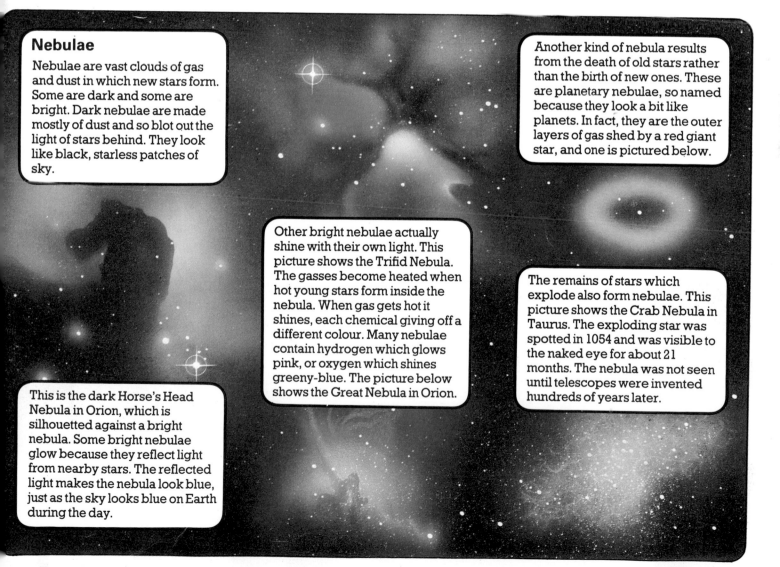

Nebulae

Nebulae are vast clouds of gas and dust in which new stars form. Some are dark and some are bright. Dark nebulae are made mostly of dust and so blot out the light of stars behind. They look like black, starless patches of sky.

This is the dark Horse's Head Nebula in Orion, which is silhouetted against a bright nebula. Some bright nebulae glow because they reflect light from nearby stars. The reflected light makes the nebula look blue, just as the sky looks blue on Earth during the day.

Other bright nebulae actually shine with their own light. This picture shows the Trifid Nebula. The gasses become heated when hot young stars form inside the nebula. When gas gets hot it shines, each chemical giving off a different colour. Many nebulae contain hydrogen which glows pink, or oxygen which shines greeny-blue. The picture below shows the Great Nebula in Orion.

Another kind of nebula results from the death of old stars rather than the birth of new ones. These are planetary nebulae, so named because they look a bit like planets. In fact, they are the outer layers of gas shed by a red giant star, and one is pictured below.

The remains of stars which explode also form nebulae. This picture shows the Crab Nebula in Taurus. The exploding star was spotted in 1054 and was visible to the naked eye for about 21 months. The nebula was not seen until telescopes were invented hundreds of years later.

Life story of the stars

Stars do not stay the same forever. They have immensely long and complex lives. Astronomers have pieced together the story of the stars by studying the many different stages which can be seen from Earth.

1 All stars are born in huge clouds of gas and dust, called nebulae. The gases and dust swirl around and form into clumps which grow larger and larger and then contract, becoming very hot and dense. Eventually, nuclear reactions begin inside and the clumps start to shine. They have become new stars.

2 New stars shine blue or white and are very bright at first. They then settle down into a long middle age and shine steadily. How long a star's middle age lasts depends upon its size. Our Sun is about half way through its 10,000 million year middle age. Dwarf stars smaller than the Sun last even longer – for about 100,000 million years. The very large giant and supergiant stars have much shorter lives of only a few million years.

3 Middle aged stars are "burning" hydrogen in nuclear reactions which occur at their centres. They eventually run out of fuel and become unstable. They cool down and swell up into red giant stars. What happens next depends upon the star's original size.

4 After the red giant stage some stars just shrink into white dwarf stars while others explode and turn into either neutron stars or black holes. These three stages are explained below.

White dwarf stars

Sun-sized stars, or smaller, swell into red giants and slowly puff their outer layers into space, forming planetary nebulae. When our Sun becomes a red giant, it will swell up by about 100 times, swallowing up the planets Mercury, Venus, Earth and possibly Mars too.

At the heart of a planetary nebula is a dying star called a white dwarf. It is very small, only the size of a planet. White dwarfs are extremely heavy and dense and generate vast forces of gravity. This is because they are the crushed cores of the original stars. The atoms collapse and become very tightly packed together. White dwarfs eventually cool down and fade.

Neutron stars

Giant and supergiant stars do not have a peaceful death. They swell into vast red supergiants but then blow up with a huge explosion called a supernova.

The supernova leaves behind a rapidly expanding, tangled nebula of gases and dust with a tiny spinning star, called a neutron star, at the centre. Some neutron stars may be only one-hundredth of the size of the Moon. They are incredibly dense and heavy and spin very fast, sending out radio waves as they rotate.

Black holes

The very largest supergiant stars are so big that after exploding as supernovae they collapse past the neutron star stage and virtually vanish from our Universe. They become black holes in space.

Black holes are tiny – only a few kilometres across. They are so heavy and dense that their gravity stops light radiating away from the surface. This means that we cannot see black holes as they do not shine.

If a black hole is part of a binary system it attracts material from its companion star. As the material is pulled into the black hole it gives off X-rays. Astronomers have discovered some mysterious X-ray sources which they believe are probably caused by black holes.

A cupful of white dwarf would weigh about 100 tonnes.

A cupful of neutron star would weigh about a million, million tonnes.

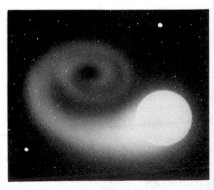

A cupful of black hole would be impossible to weigh.

The planets

If you spot a bright star in the sky which you cannot find on a star map or planisphere, you are probably looking at a planet.

Earth is one of the nine planets which are known to orbit round and round the Sun. Two of the planets, Mercury and Venus, are closer to the Sun than Earth is. Astronomers call them the inferior planets. The other planets: Mars, Jupiter, Saturn, Uranus, Neptune and Pluto, are further away from the Sun than Earth and are known as the superior planets.

Pluto was discovered in 1930 but astronomers are now beginning to wonder if it is really a planet at all and think it could be a moon which escaped from Neptune. It is also thought that there may be at least one more planet still waiting to be found.

Spotting the planets

Five of the planets – Mercury, Venus, Mars, Jupiter and Saturn – are easily visible to the naked eye. They look like bright stars until you view them through binoculars or a telescope. A star always looks like a tiny, twinkling point of light, even when magnified, but a planet looks like a steady, very small disk of light. Once you have recognised a planet you will probably be able to tell it apart from the stars by naked eye.

Finding the planets

The planets are not shown on star maps because they move slowly but continuously in relation to the fixed stars. If you watch a planet for a few weeks, this wandering will be obvious. The planets are always to be found in the constellations of the Zodiac, roughly following a line known as the ecliptic. The line of the ecliptic is shown on most star maps and planispheres. This chart shows the constellations where you will find Mars, Jupiter and Saturn over the next few years.

	1983	1984		1985		1986
Mars	Nov.-Dec. Virgo	Jan.-Aug. Libra Sept.-Oct. Sagittarius Nov. Dec. Capricornus		Jan.-Feb. Pisces Nov.-Dec. Virgo	Jan.-Feb. Scorpius Mar.-Oct. Sagittarius Nov.-Dec.Capricornus	
Jupiter	Scorpius	Sagittarius		Capricornus	Aquarius	
Saturn	Virgo	Libra		Libra	Scorpius	

Making observations

Planets do not shine with their own light but by reflecting the light of the Sun. Even so, the nearer planets are so brilliant that they are easy to spot even in lit-up city skies and when the Moon is full. It is difficult to see details on the planets though. You need to have good seeing conditions and a fairly large telescope with quite high magnification in order to see markings on Mars and Jupiter or Saturn's rings. It is still worth watching them with binoculars or even the naked eye as you can follow their movement through the stars and watch out for changes in brightness as they move.

Planets and their orbits

As Earth and the planets are all going round the Sun at different distances and speeds, their positions in relation to each other are constantly changing. Sometimes Earth is on the same side of the Sun as another planet. At other times Earth is on the opposite side of the Sun to that planet. Astronomers have named these different positions and they are shown in these diagrams. Note that they are different for the inferior and superior planets.

The various positions affect our view of the planets. They look bigger and brighter when Earth and the planet are close together – at opposition for the superior planets and around inferior conjunction for Mercury and Venus.

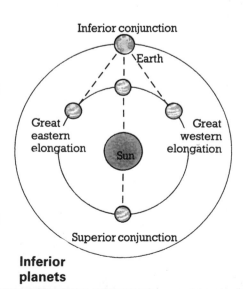

Inferior planets

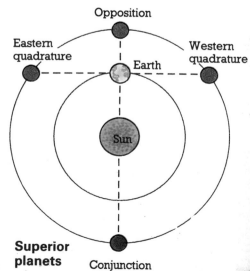

Superior planets

Outer planets

Mars, Jupiter, Saturn, Uranus, Neptune and Pluto are the superior planets that are further from the Sun than Earth is. They all orbit the Sun, and from Earth it looks as if they are moving through the fixed background of the stars. Mars, Jupiter and Saturn look like bright coloured stars that seem to change their position in relation to other stars over a few weeks.

The superior planets all move through the 12 constellations of the Zodiac, following the imaginary line of the ecliptic. A planet takes the same length of time to go once round the Zodiac as it does to orbit the Sun once. Mars takes just under two years, Jupiter almost 12 years, Saturn almost 30 years, Uranus 84 years, Neptune almost 164 years and Pluto 247 years. This gives you an idea of how slowly they move against the stars.

Backward planets

If you watch the superior planets as they slowly move across the sky, you may notice that they occasionally behave rather strangely. Usually the planets cross the sky from west to east, against the background of fixed stars. Sometimes, however, they seem to slow down, stop and then move backwards from east to west for a short time, before carrying on in the original direction. Astronomers call this "retrograde motion".

The planets don't actually stop and move backwards in space. It just looks like this from Earth. It happens because all the planets are travelling round the Sun in the same direction. Earth, on its shorter journey, catches up with them and then overtakes the superior planets. This picture shows how Earth and Mars actually move on their orbits, and the apparent movement of Mars as seen from Earth.

Jupiter, Saturn, Uranus, Neptune and Pluto move in this backward way too, seeming to pass through one constellation only to return to it for a short time a few months later.

What you see

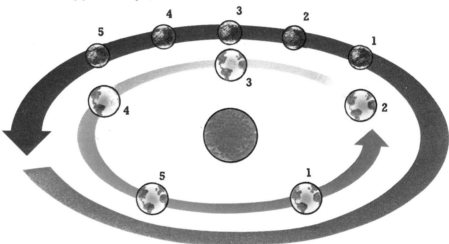

This dotted line shows how Mars seems to move across the sky in a loop over a few months

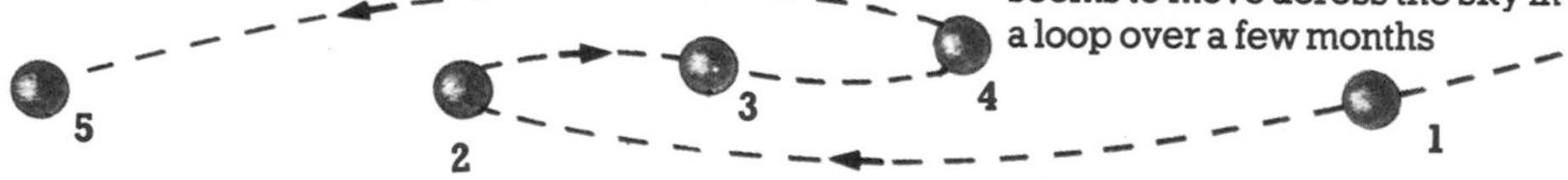

Once Earth has overtaken and passed Mars, the superior planet resumes its normal path through the sky from east to west.

As Earth catches up with Mars, the superior planet seems to slow down, stop and then move backwards in a loop.

What happens in space

Mars, the red planet

Mars looks like a bright, reddish star to the naked eye. It is always brilliant, reaching a maximum of Mag. −2.5 and not falling below about Mag. 1.5. Through binoculars, Mars is obviously disk-shaped, but surprisingly small. It can be disappointing to observe with a telescope because of its size and also because huge dust storms often cover much of the planet, obscuring any surface detail large enough to be seen from Earth. Mars is red because its rocks are coloured by rust.

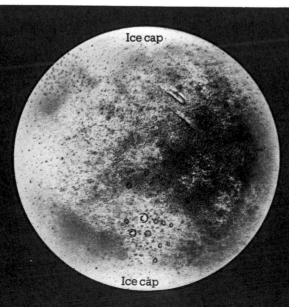

Ice cap

Ice cap

A small telescope, such as a 75mm (3in) refractor or a 110mm (4.5in) reflector, will show you the ice caps at the Martian poles. You will be able to watch them slowly shrink and grow with the changing seasons. A larger telescope will reveal more and under good conditions you may be able to see dark areas on the orange disk. These were once thought to be areas of vegetation but are now known to be features such as craters, mountains, volcanoes and deep valleys.

Jupiter, the giant planet

Jupiter is very bright, often the most brilliant white "star" in the late night sky. When it is closest to Earth, Jupiter reaches up to Mag. −2.5. It looks bright although very distant from Earth because it is extremely large and reflects a lot of sunlight. Jupiter is not a solid, rocky planet, but is made mostly of gases and liquids. It rotates very fast, taking less than 10 hours to spin round once. This rotation pulls the planet slightly out of shape, causing a flattening at the poles and a bulge around the equator. You can see this clearly through a small telescope and possibly even with binoculars.

Jupiter has many moons and three or four of them are visible with binoculars, if the seeing is good and you can keep

These light and dark belts are clouds of different chemicals.

Great Red Spot

the binoculars really steady. These main moons look like tiny pinpricks of light, lying in a straight line on either side of the globe. If you make a note of their positions each night you will see that the moons orbit round Jupiter. The nearest moons orbit fastest.

With a small telescope you can see the moons more clearly and also the dark and light coloured bands, known as belts, on the disk of the planet. A larger telescope allows you to see more belts and possibly some spots, including the largest which is called the Great Red Spot because of its size and colour. Jupiter rotates so quickly, that you can watch these features drift across the globe from right to left over a few hours.

Saturn, the ringed planet

Saturn is smaller than Jupiter and also further away, so our view of it is not as good. Even so, it is very bright with a maximum of Mag. −0.1. This planet is rather disappointing viewed through binoculars as it just looks like a slightly squashed disk. You need a telescope to see Saturn's famous system of rings at all and a fairly large one (such as a 100mm (4in) refractor or a 150mm (6in) reflector), to see them in detail. Some of the planet's moons and coloured bands and spots on the surface are also visible with a big telescope.

As Saturn orbits the Sun, our view of the rings changes. Sometimes they are

edge on and almost impossible to see. They are at their most spectacular when open towards us. The diagram below shows how Saturn looks from Earth during the course of its 29 year orbit.

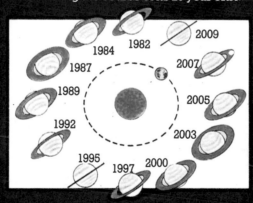

See if you can spot the shadow cast by Saturn onto its rings.

Uranus and Neptune

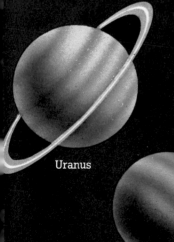

Uranus

Neptune

Uranus reaches a maximum of Mag. 5.8 and so is just visible to the naked eye, if you know where to look. Neptune can be seen with binoculars, but both of these planets are difficult to locate in the sky because they are so faint. They are gassy giants like Jupiter and Saturn but only about half their size and much further away. Even with a telescope it is not easy to make out the disk shapes of these planets, so they look very like stars.

In 1977 astronomers discovered that Uranus has rings, like Saturn's but smaller. They cannot be seen from Earth, even with the very largest telescopes but were found when Uranus "occulted" (passed directly in front of) a star. The rings made the star wink in and out of view on either side of the planet, just before and just after it was covered.

Pluto

Pluto is very small, probably smaller than our Moon. It is also very distant and so is not within range of amateur telescopes and only looks disk-shaped when seen through the largest telescope in the world.

19

Inner planets

Mercury and Venus can only be seen just before sunrise or just after sunset, never in the middle of the night. This is because they are closer to the Sun than Earth is and so always appear near to the Sun in the sky.

When observing these planets, make absolutely sure that the Sun is either fully set or not yet risen before you start looking for them. It is all too easy to catch a glimpse of the Sun accidentally and this can blind you if you are using a telescope or binoculars.

Mercury and venus move around the sky so quickly that they go through all of the constellations of the Zodiac each year. Astronomy magazines will show you where to look for these two planets each month.

It is not possible to see any details of the surfaces of Mercury or Venus. Mercury is about the same size as our Moon, which it resembles in many ways. Venus is almost the same size as Earth and has a thick atmosphere of deadly gases.

Transits

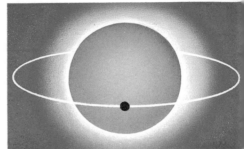

Occasionally the orbits of Earth and the inferior planets line up so that Mercury and Venus seem to cross the Sun. These are called transits.

Transits can only be seen with a telescope used in the special way for viewing the Sun. (See pages 24-25 for how to do this.) The next transit of Mercury is due on 12 November 1986; the next transit of Venus will not be until 2004.

Mercury and . . .   . . . Venus

Mercury is never very easy to see clearly as it is always near the horizon where dust, haze and turbulence make observation difficult. It also looks small, but reaches a maximum of Mag. −1.2. Venus is easy to see as it is so bright – it is the most brilliant thing in the night sky after the Moon. It reaches a maximum of Mag. −4.4, just enough to cast shadows if there are no other lights. Venus is so brilliant because it is shrouded in thick clouds which reflect the Sun's light. Unfortunately they also hide the surface and so no details of the planet can be seen from Earth, although it is close.

Phases

Mercury and Venus go through phases, like the Moon. They change in apparent size and brilliance as they change shape. The phases are invisible to the naked eye but can be seen with high power binoculars or a telescope. Mercury and Venus look smallest and least bright when full, as they are then most distant from Earth (superior conjunction), but they are not always visible in this position. The planets seem to grow bigger and brighter as they move towards Earth, but we see less and less of their lit-up sides. They are biggest and most brilliant as crescents because the planets are then closer to the Earth.

The planets get bigger and brighter as they move towards Earth.

The planets get smaller and fainter as they move away from Earth

Full phase

Half phase

Half phase

Crescent

Crescent

New phase (invisible)

The Moon

The Moon is the biggest and brightest thing in the night sky, reaching Mag. − 12.5 when full. It changes slightly in shape, position and brilliance from night to night and this makes it a very interesting object to watch. The Moon does not make any light of its own but just reflects sunlight down to Earth. It is the Earth's closest neighbour in space, only 348,000km (249,000mi) away and is about a quarter the size of the Earth.

The Moon's phases

The Moon orbits the Earth and as it goes round, different amounts of the sunlit side can be seen from Earth. These are called phases and it takes the Moon 29½ days to go through one complete cycle of phases. You can find out which phase it is at from newspapers and diaries. The various phases are visible at different times of the day and night as the Moon rises and sets 52 minutes later each day. The invisible new moon is a daytime phase and the full moon is seen throughout the night. The waxing phases are best seen in the evening and the waning after midnight.

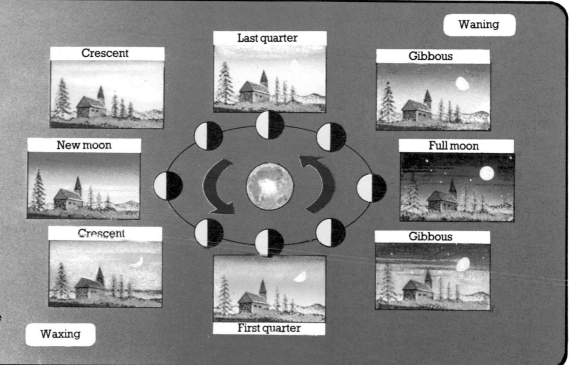

Waning

Crescent

Last quarter

Gibbous

New moon

Full moon

Crescent

Gibbous

Waxing

First quarter

The far side of the Moon

When you watch the Moon, you will notice that you always see the same side of it. This is because the Moon keeps the same half facing the Earth. No-one had seen the far side of the Moon until 1959, when a Russian spacecraft orbited the Moon and sent pictures back to Earth.

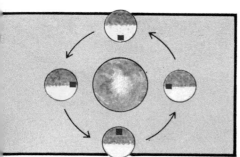

The Moon keeps the same face turned towards Earth because it spins once on its axis during one orbit of the Earth, taking 27⅓ days to do both. Astronomers call this "spin-orbit coupling" or "captured rotation". It is caused by Earth's gravity which holds the Moon in orbit and controls its rate of spin.

Slightly more than half of the Moon's surface can be seen over a period of a few months. This is because the Moon rocks very slowly and slightly in space. It seems to nod up and down from north to south and roll from east to west, giving us a peek round the edges. These tiny movements are called librations. You will only notice them if you watch the Moon carefully for some time, noting the positions of craters and other features which are close to the edges. You will see that they change slightly, with more or less in view depending on the libration. The librations occur because the Moon's spin and orbit get slightly out of step with each other. The pictures below show the librations.

Libration in latitude

This allows us to see a little more of the Moon's north and south polar regions. It happens because the Moon's axis is tilted at an angle to its orbit round the Earth.

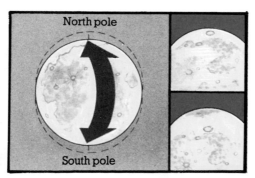

North pole

South pole

Libration in longitude

This shows us more of the surface to the east and west. It occurs because the Moon's speed changes as it goes round on its orbit, twisting the Moon from side to side slightly as seen from Earth.

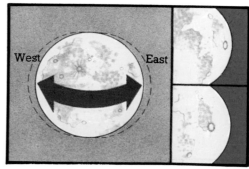

West

East

Moon map

This map shows the main features you can look for on the Moon. It has been drawn with north at the top, so it is the view that you have with the naked eye or binoculars. Most astronomical telescopes make things look upside down, with south at the top and many Moon and astronomical maps are printed like this too.

Many of the major features have both Latin names and English names. The Latin names are given here as they are the most commonly used by astronomers. You will probably find it difficult to recognize many of the features at first, but after a few observations you will begin to find your way around the Moon. It can help to study some close-up photographs too.

Observing the Moon

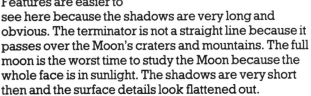

You really need to watch the Moon going through all its phases to see all the features as clearly as possible. They show up best when on the "terminator". This is the line between the sunlit half and the dark half. Features are easier to see here because the shadows are very long and obvious. The terminator is not a straight line because it passes over the Moon's craters and mountains. The full moon is the worst time to study the Moon because the whole face is in sunlight. The shadows are very short then and the surface details look flattened out.

The outer edges of the Moon are known as the "limb". What you can see on the limb depends upon where the Moon is on its orbit.

The larger your telescope and the higher the magnification you use, the more things you will see. However, even binoculars reveal many of the major features shown on this map.

Maria

These are dark areas which are the Moon's most obvious features, and make up the face of the "Man in the Moon". Ancient astronomers believed them to be seas and oceans but in fact they are flat areas of dark, volcanic rock. Mare (plural maria, pronounced MAria) is the Latin word for sea. Some maria are circular, eg Mare Imbrium and Mare Crisium, while others are irregular, eg Oceanus Procellarum.

Craters

Craters are circular depressions in the lunar surface. they often look like very deep pits but actually do not have terribly steep sides. They are bounded by gently sloping walls and many have a small peak at the centre. This picture shows how a crater would look from the side.

Craters near to the limb of the Moon usually look oval rather than circular. This is just an optical illusion due to the fact that the Moon is a sphere.

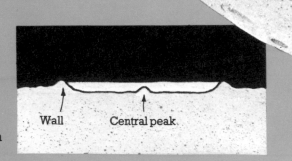

Wall   Central peak

Plato
Sinus Iridum
Sinus Roris
Aristil
Mare Imbrium
Archimede
Aristarchus
Apennine M
Kepler
Copernicus
Oceanus Procellarum
Sinus Aestuum
Grimaldi
Ptolomaeu
Riphaeus Mts
Mare Nubium
Gassendi
Tycho
Schickard
Clavius

Ray-craters

These are best seen at the full moon, unlike all other features, as they are surface deposits of bright, reflecting material. The rays stretch outwards from the craters for hundreds of kilometres. Ray-craters are thought to be the most recently formed of all craters. Tycho is the brightest of these.

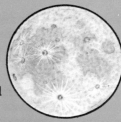

Mountains

Apart from the flat maria regions, the Moon is a very hilly place. There are many mountain ranges which can be seen from Earth with a small telescope. They look at their best when at or near the terminator. Many are named after ranges on Earth. The Apennines are the highest, with one peak soaring to over 7,500m (24,600ft).

Valleys

Like valleys on the Earth, most of those on the Moon run between mountains. Some are very deep and wide. One of the best to look for is the Alpine Valley, close to the crater Plato and the Alps mountain. Valleys and mountains on the limb make the edge of the Moon rough and bumpy.

Rills, faults and ridges

The Moon is scarred by various surface cracks and faults which were caused by mountain building, crater formation and other disturbances millions of years ago. One large rill runs between the two seas Mare Tranquillitatis and Mare Vaporum, close to the centre of the face of the Moon.

Crater chains

These are often mistaken for valleys, which they closely resemble when seen from Earth. In fact they are lines of linked craters where some of the crater walls have collapsed. One to look for is the misnamed Rheita Valley.

Transient lunar phenomena (TLPs)

TLPs are small areas of reddish coloured mist which suddenly, though very rarely, appear for a brief time on the surface of the Moon. They are usually to be seen around bright, "new" craters such as Tycho. TLPs are thought to be clouds of gas which shoot through the surface from the inside of the Moon. Until the Apollo Moon landings proved that there were moonquakes, TLPs were not taken very seriously.

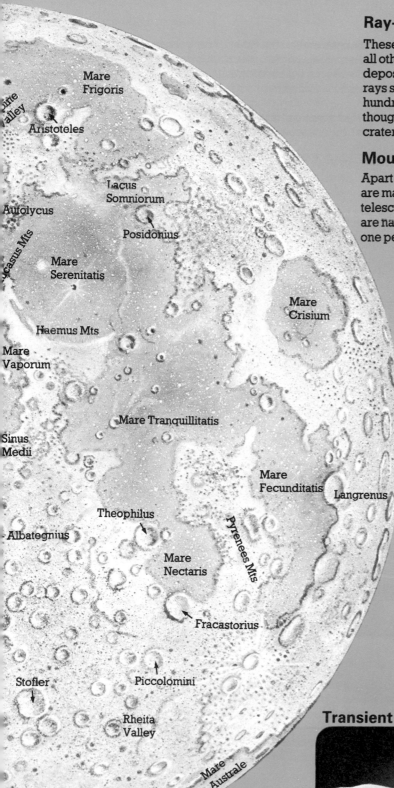

Mare Frigoris

Aristoteles

Alpine Valley

Lacus Somniorum

Autolycus

Caucasus Mts

Posidonius

Mare Serenitatis

Haemus Mts

Mare Vaporum

Mare Tranquillitatis

Mare Crisium

Sinus Medii

Mare Fecunditatis

Langrenus

Theophilus

Albategnius

Pyrenees Mts

Mare Nectaris

Fracastorius

Stofler

Piccolomini

Rheita Valley

Mare Australe

Leibnitz Mts

The Sun

The Sun is just one of the many millions of smallish yellow stars in our Galaxy. It is about 150 million km (93 million mi) away from Earth and its light takes eight minutes to reach us. As the Sun is visible on most days and, unlike the stars, can be seen as clearly from a city as from the countryside, it is an easy subject to study. However, make sure you to follow the suggestions given here when observing the Sun.

If the Sun were a double star or part of a cluster, there would be many much bigger and brighter stars visible at night and possibly even during the day.

Observing the Sun

One very important point to remember is that the Sun is dangerous. It gives off so much light and heat that you should never look at it directly, even with the naked eye. Looking directly at the Sun with binoculars or a telescope is almost certain to cause blindness. You should not even look at the sky close to the Sun with binoculars or a telescope in case you accidentally catch a glimpse of the Sun.

Some telescopes are supplied with a special "Sun filter cap" which is supposed to allow you to look directly at the Sun safely. The best thing to do with one of these is to throw it away unused. They are not really safe as there is always a chance that the hot sunlight will crack or shatter the cap while you are using it. The only safe way to observe the Sun is by projection, as shown below.

Using a telescope

To study the Sun safely all you need are binoculars or a telescope, some sheets of cardboard, sticky tape and white paper. Set up your telescope so that it is pointing towards the Sun. It is best to keep the lens cover on while you are doing this as magnified sunlight can set things alight and cause burns. If your telescope has a finder-scope, remember to keep this capped all the time too.

Tape a sheet of cardboard to the telescope to cast a shadow and hold, or rest, a sheet of white paper under the eye piece. When you uncap the lens an image of the Sun will be projected onto this paper. You can now move the paper and adjust the focus until the image is sharp and the size that you want.

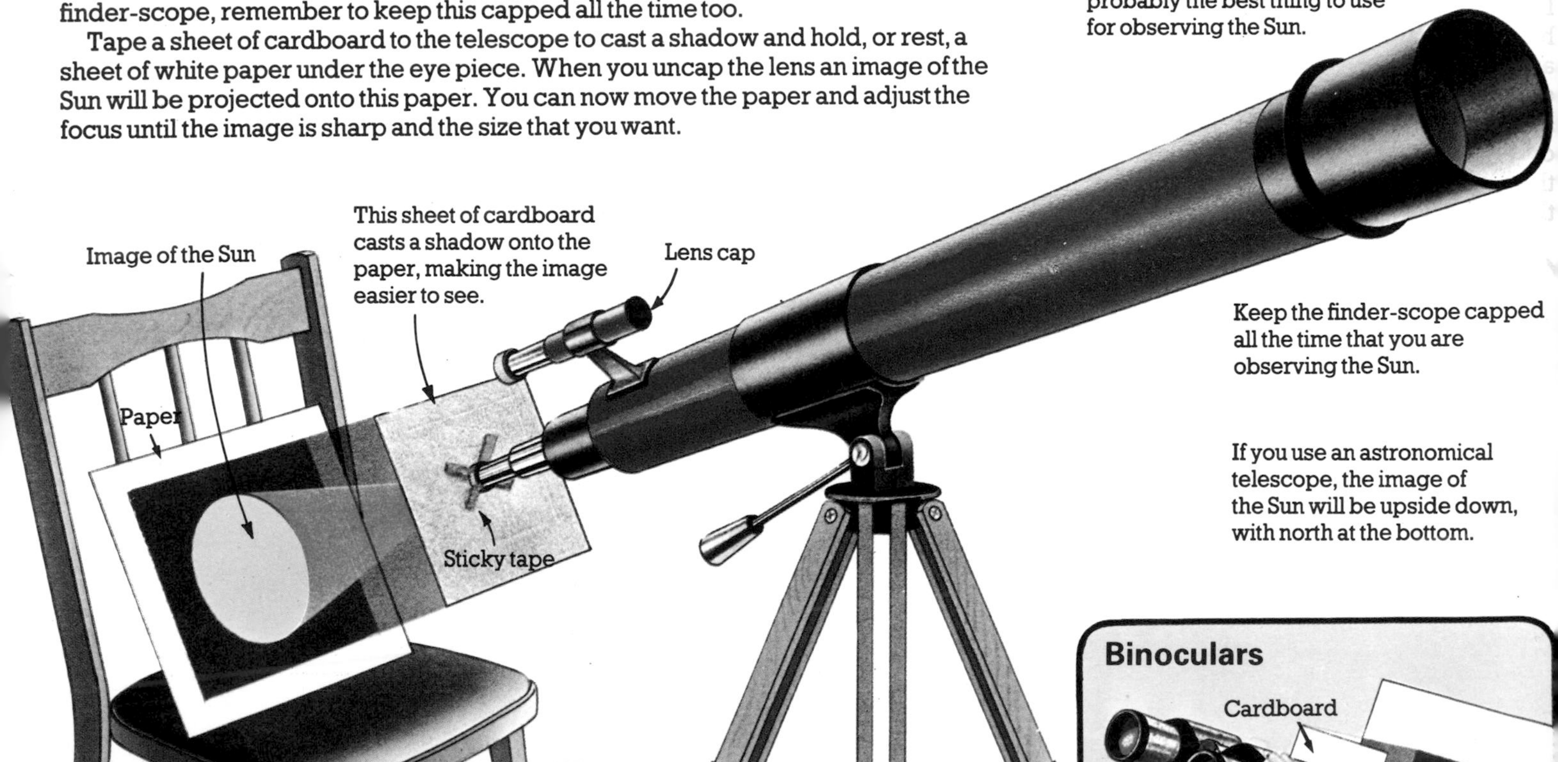

A small refracting telescope is probably the best thing to use for observing the Sun.

Image of the Sun

This sheet of cardboard casts a shadow onto the paper, making the image easier to see.

Lens cap

Paper

Sticky tape

Keep the finder-scope capped all the time that you are observing the Sun.

If you use an astronomical telescope, the image of the Sun will be upside down, with north at the bottom.

Binoculars

Cardboard

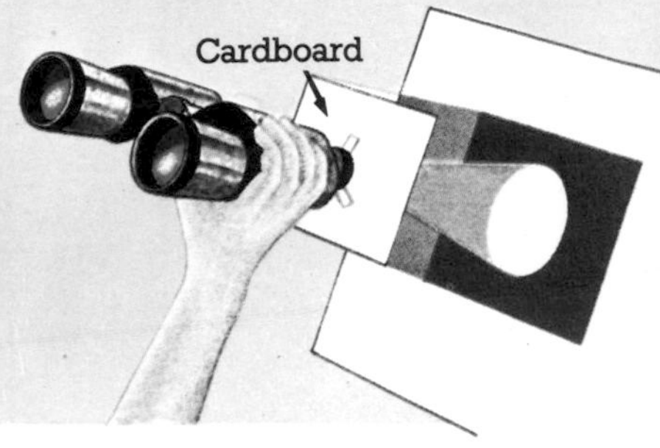

If you have binoculars, use just one of the objective lenses and keep the other capped or covered by the cardboard.

Keeping Sun records

It is a good idea to keep a record of your observations of the Sun by drawing it. Draw a circle of a convenient size, say about 12cm (4-5in) in diameter, and project an image of the Sun onto this sheet of paper so that the disk of the Sun fits into the circle. If you always use the same size circle your drawings will be to the same scale. Draw in any sunspots, flares or other things.

The part of the Sun that you see is an extremely thin layer called the photosphere. Above this is the Sun's atmosphere, which you cannot see. The outer part of the atmosphere is called the corona and this stretches far into space. It is only visible when the Sun is completely covered by the Moon at a full solar eclipse (see page 26).

The photosphere looks very mottled. This is because columns of gas keep rising to the surface and the effect is called granulation.

The Sun is very hot, about 6,000°C on the surface, but deep in the centre where nuclear reactions occur the temperature reaches a staggering 15 million°C.

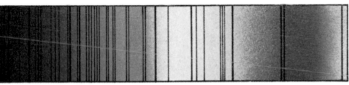

Like all stars, the Sun is a mixture of chemicals. Astronomers have identified over 70 chemicals in the Sun. They do this with an instrument called a spectroscope. Like a prism this breaks down sunlight into a spectrum of rainbow colours, but with a spectroscope it is crossed by black lines. Each set of lines is caused by a particular chemical and so astronomers "read" the lines to see which are present. The picture above shows the Sun's spectrum.

Huge eruptions of gas flare up into the Sun's atmosphere but these are not easy to see either, except at a full eclipse.

Sunspots

You will probably see a few dark spots on the projected image of the Sun. These are called sunspots and are areas of gas about 2,000°C cooler than the rest of the surface, which makes them look dark. They usually appear in groups of two large and several smaller spots and may be visible for anything between a few hours and several weeks.

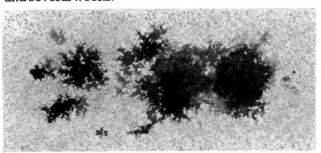

The number of sunspots on the Sun is not constant, but varies over a cycle of about 11 years. The last period of maximum sunspot activity was 1980, so the next will be 1991. The positions of the spots also varies during the cycle. At maximum most spots are near the equator, at minimum they are closer to the poles.

If you watch a sunspot group for a few days you will see it slowly moving across the Sun. What you are actually seeing is the Sun spinning on its axis. Spots close to the equator take about 27 days to go right round the Sun and those nearer the poles take a few days longer. Many spots do not last long enough to make a complete journey round the Sun. They are usually seen in the areas marked in red on this diagram of the Sun.

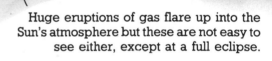

North pole

Equator

South pole

Sunspots do not always seem to be moving across the Sun in straight lines because the Earth's orbit is tilted towards the Sun. The tilt changes over the year and these pictures show the positions of the sun's poles and equator at different months.

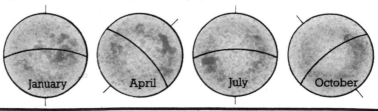

January   April   July   October

Eclipses

Most of the things to observe in the night sky are there night after night, but eclipses and occultations are not. They are occasional, fleeting events which last for just a few minutes each time. This makes them all too easy to miss if the weather is bad, or your timing is inaccurate. Eclipses and occultations occur as a result of the movements of the Moon and planets, including Earth, around the Sun.

Why eclipses happen

No eclipse
Solar eclipse
Lunar eclipse
No eclipse

Eclipses of the Sun and Moon happen when the Earth and the Moon get in the way of each other's shadows. This only happens occasionally, as the Moon's orbit round Earth is tilted at an angle to the Earth's orbit round the Sun. Eclipses of the Sun only happen when the Moon is at the new phase and eclipses of the Moon only happen when it is at the full phase.

Solar eclipses

The most dramatic and unusual kind of eclipse is a total eclipse of the Sun. Astronomers travel all over the world to see them as they are the only time when the Sun's outer atmospere, the corona, is visible without special equipment. Solar eclipses can only be seen from a small area of the Earth, which is different each time. They are also very brief. The longest that "totality" (the time that the Sun is covered) can last is seven minutes, but most are much shorter and some last for only a few seconds. We see total solar eclipses only because the Sun and Moon look about the same size in the sky. The Sun is really 400 times bigger than the Moon but it is also 400 times further away.

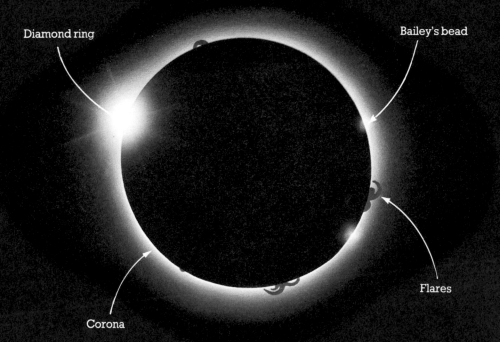

Diamond ring

Bailey's bead

Corona

Flares

Moon shadow

Solar eclipses happen when the Moon passes directly between the Sun and Earth so that its shadow lands on Earth. The eclipse can only be seen from the places covered by the shadow, which is always very narrow. The shadow is made up of two parts, a dark inner shadow called the umbra and a fainter outer shadow, the penumbra.

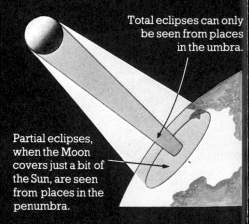

Total eclipses can only be seen from places in the umbra.

Partial eclipses, when the Moon covers just a bit of the Sun, are seen from places in the penumbra.

Annular eclipse

Another kind of eclipse is an annular eclipse which happens when the Moon is at its most distant from Earth and looks smaller than the Sun. It cannot quite cover the Sun, even if they line up exactly. A ring of Sun is visible all round the edge of the Moon, so the corona cannot be seen.

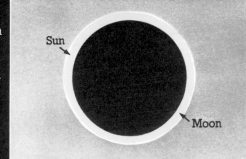

Sun

Moon

The best way to see the Sun during an eclipse is by projecting an image of it, as shown on page 24. Do not be tempted to look at the Sun through smoked glass, as some newspapers may suggest, as this lets through dangerous rays which harm your eyes.

You should be able to see the thin gases of the corona streaming far out into space and you may be able to spot some flares poking out beyond the dark disk of the Moon. As the Moon does not have a smooth surface but is very mountainous, slivers of sunlight shine out round the edges, through the valleys. These are called "Bailey's Beads" after the astronomer who discovered them. As the Sun enters and leaves totality, a big ray of sunlight may shine out creating an effect known as the "diamond ring".

Lunar eclipses

Eclipses of the Moon happen when the Sun, Earth and Moon line up at full phase so that Earth's shadow falls on the Moon. A lunar eclipse can be seen from the whole of the night side of Earth.

The Moon does not disappear completely when eclipsed, but grows darker and changes colour, usually going a deep coppery red. Lunar eclipses can last for up to an hour and three quarters.

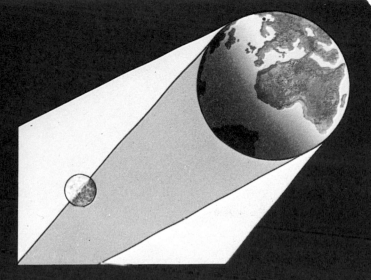

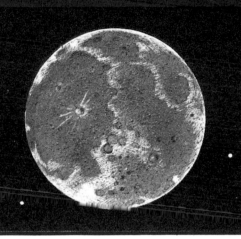

Earth's shadow is made up of a dark umbra and fainter penumbra. You will only see a total eclipse of the Moon when it is covered by the umbra. If only part of the Moon passes through the umbra you see a partial eclipse. If the Moon misses the umbra altogether and just goes through the penumbra, an eclipse still takes place but is much less noticeable as the Moon does not get very much darker or change in colour a great deal.

Occultations

During their journeys across the sky, the Moon and planets occasionally move in front of and eclipse stars. This is called occultation. Occultations by the Moon are more frequent than occultations by planets as the Moon looks much larger and moves faster. Sometimes the Moon occults a planet and planets even occult each other, although this is much rarer.

You can find out when occultations are going to take place from astronomical societies or magazines. Occultations are not as common as you might expect, looking at the vast numbers of stars in the sky. Only stars in the constellations of the Zodiac, close to the line of the ecliptic, can be occulted. The really bright stars in this position are Antares, Aldebaran, Spica and Regulus.

A star vanishes instantly when occulted by the Moon. One second it is there, the next it has gone, so it is easy to miss unless you are watching carefully. Sometimes a star vanishes but then unexpectedly reappears almost immediately, before vanishing again. This happens when a star is first hidden by a mountain and then shines out through the next valley. When a

double star system is occulted it seems to fade a little just before going behind the Moon, because one of the stars is hidden before the other, cutting down the combined light.

As planets are not points of light like stars, but disks, it can take up to a few seconds for the Moon to completely cover them during an occultation.

Grazing occultations

Occasionally a star or planet is not completely covered by the Moon but just grazes the edge, or limb. It flickers in and out of view as it goes behind lunar mountains and then shines out through the valleys in between.

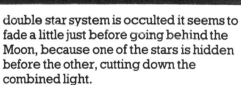

If you have a list of future occultations from an astronomical society, it will probably also give you a figure called a "position angle" for each occultation. This tells you where the star will emerge from behind the Moon at the end of the occultation. The angle is measured in degrees from the north pole.

Comets and meteors

A big brilliant comet or a heavy shower of bright meteors are two of the most exciting sights in the night sky, and they are often unpredictable in appearance. This makes them especially interesting for amateur astronomers to study. Professionals are usually too busy working on specialist projects to search for the arrival of a new comet or count the rate of falls in a meteor shower.

If you want to search the sky for comets and meteors choose a dark, moonless night. Binoculars or a small telescope with low magnification are the best things to use as you need a wide field of view and these are often faint fuzzy objects.

Most comets are not very spectacular sights. Many are too faint to be seen with binoculars and look like woolly smudges of faint light even with a telescope. Although some comets are huge, brilliant and impressive, they are not as substantial as they look. Astronomers have called comets "dirty snowballs in space" as they are made from ice, dust, bits of rock and frozen chemicals. They consist of a head and a long tail, or even two. Earth could go right through a comet's tail without coming to any harm. The tails are also quite transparent and stars are visible through them.

Comets in space

Comets orbit round the Sun like planets but have very elongated, elliptical orbits which take them close to the Sun but also very far from it, often beyond the solar system altogether.

A comet can take many thousands of years to complete one orbit, but some appear every few years or decades. These are called regular or periodic comets. The famous Halley's Comet is periodic, returning every 76 years. It is due again in 1986.
About 20 comets come close to Earth every year, but big, bright comets that can be seen with the naked eye appear only about once every ten years or so. The last really good one was Comet West in 1975, so there could be another some time soon. A brilliant comet may be visible in the sky for many weeks or even months, but most ordinary comets can be seen for just a few days.

Comets are invisible until they get quite close to the Sun. The Sun's heat melts the frozen chemicals which glow as they get hot, in the same way as gases in a fluorescent light.

Comet's orbits are usually at an angle to the plane of the solar system.

Solar system

The dust in a comet also helps to make it bright. It shines and glitters by reflecting sunlight.

A comet's tail is actually formed by the Sun which blows out the gases and dust with a stream of radiation called solar wind. The tails always point away from the sun, no matter what direction the comet is moving in, because of this.

Lots of comets have two tails: a straight one made of glowing gas and a curved one made of dust. They are often hundreds of millions of kilometres long. The biggest may be long enough to stretch from the Sun, beyond Earth to Mars.

Meteors

Meteors are streaks of light which whizz across the sky, making a tiny flash that lasts for a second or less. They are caused by minute pieces of space dust, called meteoroids, which drop into Earth's atmosphere and burn as they fall through the air. Most meteors are quite faint, Mag. 3 or less, but some are brighter. You are likely to see a few meteors on any dark night but the best time to look is after midnight. If you are in the northern hemisphere look high in the sky to the east and south east, in the southern hemisphere look west and north west.

Fireballs

Most meteoroids vaporize without getting anywhere near the ground, but a few are large enough to survive the fall. These large ones make very bright, long streaks of light which can last for up to a minute and even make a bang. They are known as fireballs and are rather rare.

Once a meteroid has landed on Earth it is called a meteorite. They are very interesting to astronomers as they provide us with samples of rock from space. Most are made of rock or iron, or a mixture of both.

Meteors also fall in showers at regular times of the year. They are caused by comets which leave a trail of dust along their orbits. Earth crosses the orbits of old comets at the same times each year so astronomers know when showers will occur, though it is impossible to predict how heavy or bright the meteors will be. Showers often last for several nights and at the peak there may be more than 60 meteors an hour. This picture shows how a shower would look on a long exposure photograph. See page 31 for the dates of some showers.

Satellites

When out observing you may see a spot of light moving quickly across the sky. This is probably an artificial satellite. There are thousands orbiting the Earth and some newspapers give the rising and setting times of the brighter ones. Satellites often seem to flash on and off because they rotate and glint in the Sun.

Aurorae

If you live in the far north or south you will be lucky enough to see the aurora. These are shimmering, glowing curtains of coloured lights that appear in the sky. They are caused by electrically charged particles of solar wind which get trapped by Earth's magnetic field and react with the atmosphere.

Zodiacal light

At and near to the equator a faint cone-shaped area of light can sometimes be seen in the night sky. It is called the Zodiacal Light and is best seen just after sunset in March or after sunrise in September. It is caused by sunlight reflecting on dust in space, beyond the Earth's atmosphere.

Going further

If you want to become a professional astronomer you will need to be good at mathematics and physics and to study for a degree at university. Modern astronomy involves many sciences and so there are engineers building space probes, technicians working radio and optical telescopes, astrophysicists analyzing the nature of the stars and computer experts writing and running astronomy programs. Most research is being carried out on recent discoveries such as black holes, the size and beginnings of the Universe and quasars – which are thought to be very distant young galaxies. All of this requires specialized and expensive equipment, yet with just a pair of binoculars and a star map, you can still explore space from your own home.

Astronomers carry out most of their studies at observatories. There are several which house giant optical telescopes that focus light onto electronic detectors or photographic film. Astronomers today spend very little, if any, time actually peering into space themselves.

There are also many radio telescopes which provide a picture of the Universe using radio waves instead of light waves.

Spaceflight has also allowed astronomers to put telescopes into space and even to send probes to the planets in our solar system.

All of this new information has to be analyzed and astronomers use powerful computers to help them in their work. The most modern equipment does not use photographic film, but video tapes, and the pictures and information are displayed on a special tv screen.

Spotter's guide to the sky

These charts list some examples of the kinds of stars and other sights which are mentioned in this book. You will be able to find many of the individual stars marked on the maps on pages 6 and 7. You will need a larger and more detailed star chart to find some of the less brilliant stars, which may only be visible with a telescope anyway. Distances are given in light years (LY) and you can look up a star's colour by checking its spectral type against the chart on page 12.

The brightest stars

Star	Constellation	Mag.	Distance	Spectral Type
Sirius	Canis Major	−1.5	8.7	A
Canopus	Carina	−0.7	181	F
Alpha Centauri	Centaurus	−0.3	4.2	G
Arcturus	Boötes	−0.1	35.9	K
Vega	Lyra	0.0	26.4	A
Capella	Auriga.	0.1	45.6	G
Rigel	Orion	0.1	880	B
Procyon	Canis Minor	0.3	11.4	F
Achernar	Eridanus	0.5	78	B
Beta Centauri	Centaurus	0.6	423.8	B
Altair	Aquila	0.7	16.4	A

Double stars

Star	Constellation	Mags.
Alpha Capricorni	Capricornus	4, 4.5
Beta Capricorni	Capricornus	3.5, 6
Beta Cygni (Albireo)	Cygnus	3, 5
Nu Draconis	Draco	5, 5
Alpha Librae	Libra	3, 5
Zeta Lyrae	Lyra	4, 5
Epsilon Lyrae	Lyra	4.5, 5
Theta Orionis (4 stars)	Orion	5-8
Theta Tauri	Taurus	4, 4.5
Zeta Ursae Majoris (Mizar and Alcor)	Ursa Major	2, 4

The nearest stars

Star	Constellation	Mag.	Distance	Spectral Type
Proxima Centauri	Centaurus	11.1	4.2	M
Alpha Centauri	Centaurus	−0.3	4.3	G
Barnard's Star	Orphiuchus	9.5	5.9	M
Lalande 21185		7.5	8.2	M
Sirius	Canis Major	−1.5	8.7	A
UV Ceti	Cetus	12.4	8.7	M
Ross 154		10.6	9.4	M
Ross 248		12.3	10.3	M
Epsilon Eridani	Eridanus	3.7	10.8	K

Variable stars

Star	Constellation	Mag.	Period
Epsilon Aurigae	Auriga	3.3-4.1	27 years
Alpha Cassiopeiae	Cassiopeia	2.2-3.1	irregular
Gamma Cassiopeiae	Cassiopeia	1.6-3	irregular
Delta Cephei	Cepheus	3.6-4.3	5 days 9 hours
Omicron Ceti (Mira)	Cetus	2-10	331 days
Eta Geminorum	Gemini	3.1-4.0	231 days
Alpha Herculis	Hercules	3.1-3.9	irregular
Beta Lyrae	Lyra	3.4-4.3	12 days 22 hours
Beta Persei (Algol)	Perseus	2.2-3.5	2 days 21 hours
Alpha Orionis (Betelgeuse)	Orion	0.4-1.3	irregular

If you have a home computer you can buy programs to help you with your astronomy. One program acts as a kind of telescope, showing which stars can be seen in particular parts of the sky at different magnifications. Your local or national astronomical society will be able to put you in touch with astrocomputing societies whose members write and exchange useful programs.

Astronomical societies

Here are the addresses of some national astronomical societies. They will be able to put you in touch with local groups in your area.

Britain
Junior Astronomical Society, 58 Vaughan Gardens, Ilford, Essex IG1 3PD.
British Astronomical Association, Burlington House, Piccadilly, London W1V 0NL.

USA
Astronomical League, PO Box 3332, Des Moines, Iowa 50316.

Canada
Royal Astronomical Society of Canada, 124 Merton Street, Toronto, Ontario M4S 2Z2.

Australia
Astronomical Society of New South Wales, PO Box 208, Eastwood, New South Wales 2122.
Astronomical Society of South Australia, PO Box 199, Adelaide, South Australia 5001.

New Zealand
Royal Astronomical Society of New Zealand, PO Box 3181, Wellington C1.

Books to read

Here are some books which will help you with astronomy.

Spotter's Guide to the Night Sky
Nigel Henbest (Usborne)

How to be an Astronomer
Robin Scagell (Macdonald)

The Young Astronomer's Handbook
Ian Ridpath (Hamlyn)

The Practical Astronomer
Colin Ronan (Pan)

The Atlas of the Universe
Patrick Moore (Mitchell Beazley)

The Guinness Book of Astronomy Facts and Feats
Patrick Moore (Guinness)

Astronomy with Binoculars
James Muirden (Faber)

Astronomy: An Introduction
Jacqueline Mitton (Faber)

All of the galaxies, nebulae and star clusters have been mapped and given an identifying number, such as M31 or NGC 869. The letters in front of the number show which list or catalogue the object can be found in, some are in both. "M" numbers refer to a catalogue made in the 18th century by a French astronomer named Messier. "NGC" numbers refer to the more modern New General Catalogue. Some of the brighter ones also have names and can be found on detailed star charts.

Star clusters

No.	Constellation	Mag.	Type
M44 (Praesepe)	Cancer	4	open
M41	Canis Major	5	open
Omega	Centaurus	4	globular
NGC 4755 (Jewel Box)	Crux	5	open
M35	Gemini	5	open
M13	Hercules	6	globular
NGC 869 NGC 884	Perseus (Double cluster)	4	open
M45 (Pleiades)	Taurus	1.5	open
M47	Puppis	6	open
NGC 104	Tucana	4	globular
M22	Sagittarius	5	globular
M7	Scorpius	3	open

Nebulae

No.	Constellation	Name	Type
NGC 7293	Aquarius	Helix	planetary
	Crux	Coalsack	dark
NGC 2070	Doradus	Tarantula	bright
M42	Orion	Great Nebula	bright
M8	Sagittarius	Lagoon	bright
M20	Sagittarius	Trifid	bright
M17	Sagittarius	Omega	bright

Galaxies

No.	Constellation	Name	Type
	Dorado	Large Magellanic Cloud	irregular
	Tucana	Small Magellanic Cloud	irregular
M31	Andromeda	Great Spiral Galaxy	spiral
M33	Triangulum		spiral

Annual meteor showers

Dates visible	Name	Constellation
January 1-6	Quadrantids	Boötes
April 19-24	Lyrids	Lyra
May 1-8	Eta Aquarids	Aquarius
July 25-August 18	Perseids	Perseus
October 16-21	Orionids	Orion
October 20-November 30	Taurids	Taurus
December 7-15	Geminids	Gemini

Astronomical symbols

Astronomers also use special symbols to represent the Sun, Moon and planets and the 12 constellations of the Zodiac.

☉ Sun	♅ Uranus	♊ Gemini
☽ Moon	♆ Neptune	♋ Cancer
☿ Mercury	♇ Pluto	♌ Leo
♀ Venus		♍ Virgo
⊕ Earth	♒ Aquarius	♎ Libra
♂ Mars	♓ Pisces	♏ Scorpius
♃ Jupiter	♈ Aries	♐ Sagittarius
♄ Saturn	♉ Taurus	♑ Capricornus

Index

The names of individual stars are shown in *italics* and the names of constellations are in **bold** type.

absolute magnitude, 11, 12, 13
Achenar, 12
Alcor, 13
Aldebaran, 12, 27
Algol, 13
Altair, 12
altazimuth mount, 5
Andromeda, 14
Andromeda Galaxy, 14
Antares, 12, 27
apparent magnitude, 11, 13
Aquarius, 17
Aquila, 7
Arcturus, 12
astronomical symbols, 31
aurorae, 29

Bailey's beads, 26
Barlow Lens, 5
Big Dipper, 6
binary star systems, 13, 16, 24, 27
binoculars, 2, 3, 4, 11, 20, 24
black holes, 16, 30
bright nebulae, 15

Canis Major, 6, 7
Canopus, 12
Capella, 12
Capricornus, 17
captured rotation, 21
Cassiopeia, 7
celestial sphere, 8, 9, 10
Cetus, 13
circumpolar stars, 9, 10
comets, 4, 28, 29
Comet West, 28
computers, 30
conjunctions, 17
constellations, 2, 3, 4, 6, 7, 11, 18, 31
corona, 25, 26
Crab Nebula, 15
craters, 22, 23
Crux, 7
Cygnus, 7, 11

dark nebulae, 15
Declination, 9
Deneb, 11
diamond ring effect, 26
double stars, 13, 24, 27, 30
dwarf stars, 12, 16

Earth, 10, 11, 12, 17, 18, 20, 26
eclipses, 26-27
ecliptic (line of), 17, 18, 27
equatorial mount, 5

field of view, 4, 5
finder-scope, 5, 24
fireballs, 29
first point of Aries, 9
flares (solar), 24, 25, 26

galaxies, 4, 14, 31
Galaxy the, 14, 15, 24
Gemini, 7
giant stars, 12, 16
globular clusters, 15, 31
granulation (solar), 25
Great Bear, 6
Great Nebula in Orion, 15
Great Red Spot, 19
Greek alphabet, 6, 7

Halley's Comet, 28
Horse's Head Nebula, 15

inferior planets, 17, 20
inner planets, 17, 20

Jupiter, 17, 18, 19

Libra, 17
librations, 21
light years, 11, 15, 30
limb (of the Moon), 22, 23, 27
line of the ecliptic, 17, 18, 27
Local Group (of galaxies), 14

Magellanic Clouds, 14
magnification, 3, 4, 5, 17, 28
magnitude, 11, 12, 13, 14, 18, 19, 20,
    21, 29
maria, 22
Mars, 16, 17, 18, 28
Mercury, 16, 17, 20
Messier catalogue, 31
meteorites, 29
meteoroids, 29
meteors, 28, 29, 31
Milky Way, 14
Mira, 13
Mizar, 13
Moon, 2, 16, 19, 20, 21-23, 26, 27
moonquakes, 23
multiple star systems, 13

nebulae, 4, 14, 15, 16, 31
Neptune, 17, 18, 19
neutron stars, 16
New General Catalogue, 31
night-adapted sight, 2
novae, 4, 13
nuclear reactions, 13, 16, 25

observing sites, 3
occultations, 19, 26, 27
open clusters, 15
optical double stars, 13
orbits:
    comets, 28
    Moon, 21
    planets, 17
Orion, 4, 7, 11, 13, 15
outer planets, 17, 18, 19

Pegasus, 7
penumbra, 26, 27
Perseus, 13
phases:
    Mercury, 20
    Moon, 21, 22, 23
    Venus, 20
photographs, 8, 14, 22, 30
photosphere (solar), 25
Pisces, 17
planetary nebulae, 15, 16
planets, 2, 17-19, 20, 26, 27, 28
planisphere, 2, 17
Pleiades, 15
Plough, 6, 13
Pluto, 17, 18, 19
Pollux, 12
Procyon, 12
Proxima Centauri, 11
pulsating variable stars, 13

quasars, 30

radio telescopes, 30
radio waves, 16, 30
ray-craters, 23
red giant stars, 13, 15, 16
Regulus, 27
retrograde motion, 18
Rigel, 12
Right Ascension, 9

Sagittarius, 17
satellites, 29
Saturn, 17, 18, 19
Scorpius, 17
seasonal stars, 10
seeing conditions, 3, 14, 17
setting circles, 9
Sirius, 11, 12
solar system, 11, 17, 28, 29
spectral types, 12, 30
spectroscope, 25
spectrum (solar), 25
Spica, 12, 27
spin-orbit coupling, 21
star clusters, 14, 15, 24, 31
star colours, 3, 8, 12, 16, 30
star diagonal eye piece, 5
star maps, 2, 6-7, 9, 14, 17, 30
star names, 6-7
star size, 12, 13
star temperature, 12, 13
starlight, 3, 11, 12
Sun, 10, 12, 13, 14, 16, 17, 18, 20,
    24-25, 26, 27, 28
sunspots, 24, 25
supergiant stars, 12, 16
superior planets, 17, 18-19
supernovae, 16

Taurus, 15
telescopes, 2, 5, 11, 14, 18, 20, 24
    catadioptric, 5
    newtonian, 5
    radio, 30
    reflecting, 5, 18
    refracting, 5, 18, 24
    terrestrial, 4
Telescopium, 6
terminator (lunar), 22, 23
Theta Orionis, 13
transient lunar phenomena, 23
transits, 20
Trapezium, 13
Trifid Nebula, 15
tripods, 4, 5, 8
turbulence, 3, 20

umbra, 26, 27
Universal Time, 3
Universe, 14, 16, 30
Uranus, 17, 18, 19
Ursa Major, 6, 7

variable stars, 13, 30
Venus, 16, 17, 20
Virgo, 7, 14, 17

waning, 21
waxing, 21
white dwarf stars, 13, 16

X-rays, 16

Zodiac, 17, 18, 20, 27, 31
Zodiacal light, 29
Zeta Orionis, 12

First published in 1983 by Usborne Publishing
Ltd, 20 Garrick Street, London WC2E 9BJ.
copyright © 1983 Usborne Publishing Ltd.

PRINTED IN BELGIUM BY

INTERNATIONAL BOOK PRODUCTION